Seven  of the World

SOUTH AMERICA

By Tracy Vonder Brink

A Crabtree Crown Book

School-to-Home Support for Caregivers and Teachers

This appealing book is designed to teach students about core subject areas. Students will build upon what they already know about the subject, and engage in topics that they want to learn more about. Here are a few guiding questions to help readers build their comprehensions skills. Possible answers appear here in red.

Before Reading:

What do I know about South America?

- *I know South America is a continent.*
- *I know the Amazon rain forest is in South America.*

What do I want to learn about this topic?

- *I want to know how many countries are in South America.*
- *I want to learn about animals that live in the Amazon rain forest.*

During Reading:

I'm curious to know...

- *I'm curious to know what kind of foods South Americans eat.*
- *I'm curious to know what sports South Americans enjoy.*

How is this like something I already know?

- *I know what foods people who live near me eat.*
- *I know what sports I like to play.*

After Reading:

What was the author trying to teach me?

- *The author was trying to teach me what kind of landforms South America has.*
- *The author was trying to teach me about South American countries.*

How did the photographs and captions help me understand more?

- *The photographs helped me picture South America.*
- *The captions gave me extra information.*

TABLE OF CONTENTS

CHAPTER 1
Get to Know South America. 4

CHAPTER 2
Landforms and Climate 8

CHAPTER 3
Natural Resources. 14

CHAPTER 4
Plants and Animals. 16

CHAPTER 5
Countries and Cities 22

CHAPTER 6
Culture and People 26

GLOSSARY. 30

INDEX 31

COMPREHENSION QUESTIONS. 31

ABOUT THE AUTHOR 32

CHAPTER 1
GET TO KNOW SOUTH AMERICA

What continent has the longest mountain range in the world? Where do toucans fly and jaguars hunt? Where do more than 400 million people live?

South America!

The **equator** runs through South America. South America is south of North America. A narrow strip of land called the Isthmus of Panama connects the two. South America is north of Antarctica.

The world has seven continents. South America is the fourth largest.

OCEANS AND ISLANDS

The Atlantic Ocean **borders** South America's eastern coast. The Pacific Ocean splashes against its west. A waterway known as The Drake Passage is between South America and Antarctica. The Atlantic and Pacific Oceans meet in the Drake Passage.

The Drake Passage has some of the roughest waters in the world. Hundreds of shipwrecks have happened there.

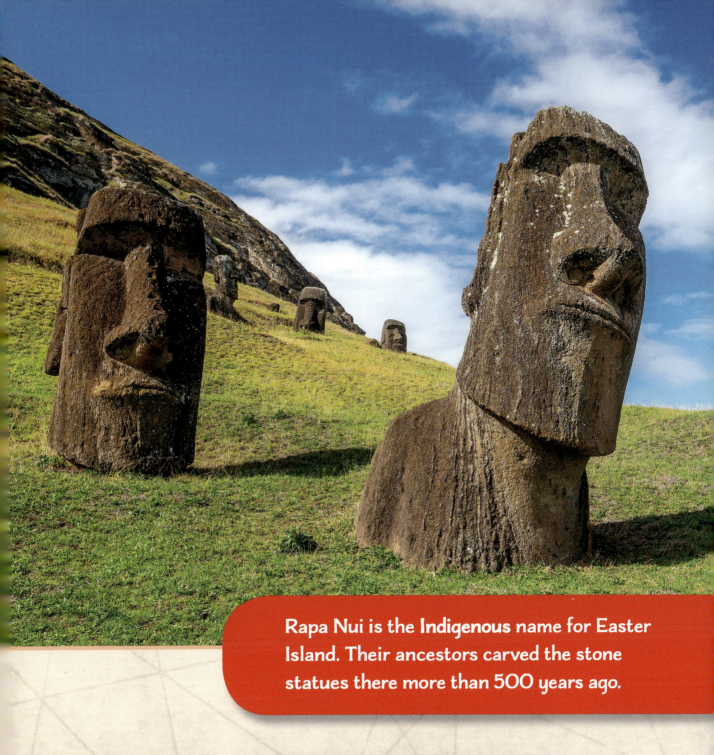

Rapa Nui is the Indigenous name for Easter Island. Their ancestors carved the stone statues there more than 500 years ago.

South America has fewer islands than other continents. But the Galápagos Islands, off its western coast, are famous for wildlife. Easter Island is known for its giant stone statues. It is also off of South America's western coast.

CHAPTER 2
LANDFORMS AND CLIMATE

South America has a major mountain chain. It has **plains** and deserts. Its river systems cover almost all of the continent. The Amazon rain forest is also part of South America.

The sources of the Amazon River begin in the Andes. The mountain chain also has four volcano zones.

MOUNTAINS

The Andes Mountains run from the north to the south along South America's entire western coast. The Andes stretch across seven countries. They are the longest mountain chain in the world.

DESERTS AND PLAINS

South America's deserts are found along its western coast. The Atacama Desert is the world's driest non-polar desert. It rains as little as 0.04 inches (1 mm) in a year. The Pampas is one of the largest plains in the world. The Pampas cover about 295,000 square miles (764,000 square km).

Scientists think the Atacama Desert might be like Mars. They study the Atacama to see how life survives in a place without water.

The Amazon River is the widest river in the world. It also carries more water than any other river.

WATERS

The Amazon River is South America's longest river. It is also one of the longest in the world. Brazil's Paraná River joins the Uruguay River to become a larger river called the Río de la Plata. Lake Titicaca is the largest lake in South America. The lake is in the Andes Mountains.

THE AMAZON RAIN FOREST

The Amazon rain forest is the world's largest tropical rain forest. It stretches through nine countries. Its trees and other plants put out the oxygen living things breathe. The rain forest plants draw in **carbon dioxide**, a waste gas.

CLIMATE

South America's **climate** is generally warm and wet. The northern areas around the equator stay sunny and hot all year. The central part of the continent is drier. The high Andes mountains in the west are snowy and cold.

CHAPTER 3
NATURAL RESOURCES

South America is one of the world's major producers of oil and natural gas. Oil and natural gas are important sources of fuel. The continent has metals such as iron, tin, and copper. Beautiful gemstones are also found in South America. Colombia is known for its emeralds.

Emeralds come from a mineral called beryl. Most Colombian emeralds are mined in the eastern Andes mountains.

Coffee beans are really the seeds of a berry that grow on a flowering bush.

Many crops grow well in the South American tropics. Brazil produces the most coffee in the world. Pineapple, papaya, and guava also come from the continent. Corn and soybeans grow on the plains. Herds of cattle roam the Pampas. Brazil and Argentina are leading producers of beef.

CHAPTER 4
PLANTS AND ANIMALS

Heliconia flowers are sometimes called "lobster claws."

Sap from rubber trees is used to make rubber.

PLANTS

Plants thrive in many parts of South America. Grasses fill the Pampas, but few trees grow there. Cactus are found in some deserts. The Amazon rain forest is home to more plant **species** than anywhere else in the world.

Many trees grow in the Amazon rain forest. Palm trees, rubber trees, and Brazil nut trees reach toward the sky. Vines wrap around tree trunks, and ferns sprout on the forest floor. Orchid and heliconia flowers bloom.

ANIMALS OF THE AMAZON RAIN FOREST

The Amazon rain forest is filled with animals. Tiny poison dart frogs live there. Their bright colors warn their skin is poisonous. Hummingbirds sip from flowers and toucans feast on fruit. Boa constrictors wind their way through the trees. Jaguars hunt day and night.

The Amazon rain forest is in danger. Human activities and forest fires destroy the homes of plants and animals. But some groups and countries are working to save it.

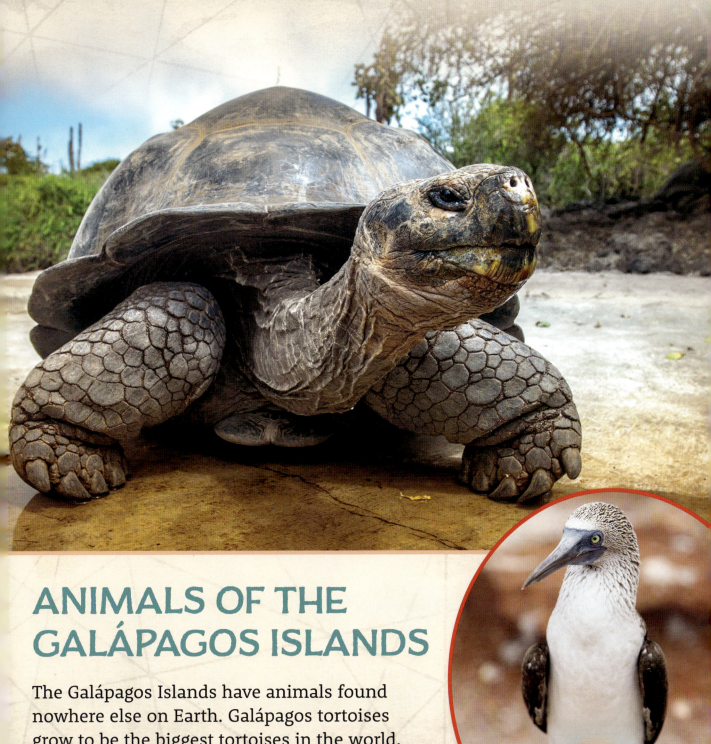

ANIMALS OF THE GALÁPAGOS ISLANDS

The Galápagos Islands have animals found nowhere else on Earth. Galápagos tortoises grow to be the biggest tortoises in the world. They may live to be a hundred years old. Marine iguanas are the only lizard that lives on land but feeds in the sea. Blue-footed boobies show off their brightly colored feet to attract a mate.

ANIMALS OF THE PAMPAS

Much of the Pampas has been taken over for cattle ranching, but some unique animals still live there. Rhea birds run through the grassland. These large birds cannot fly. Pampas deer blend into brown grasses. Pampas foxes hunt rabbits and other small animals.

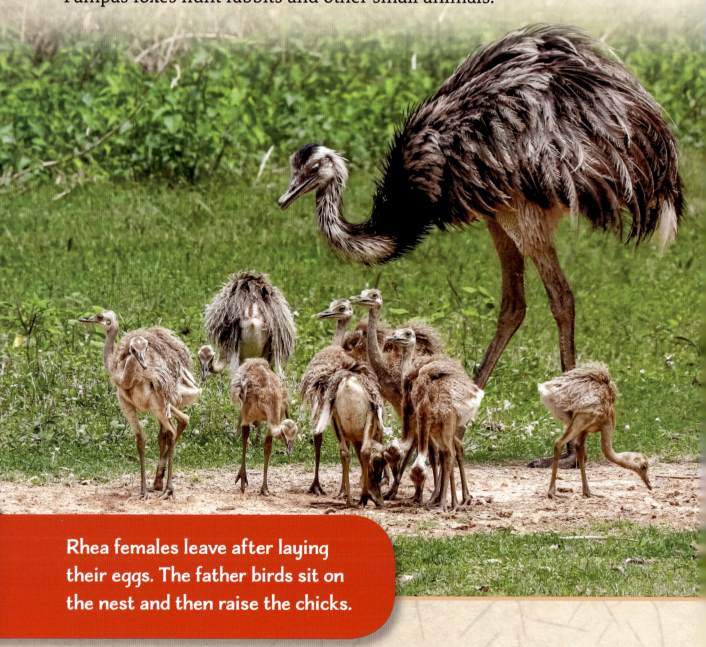

Rhea females leave after laying their eggs. The father birds sit on the nest and then raise the chicks.

The spectacled bear is named for the markings around its eyes that make it look like it's wearing glasses.

ANIMALS OF THE ANDES

Different animals call the Andes Mountains home. The spectacled bear is the only South American bear. Llamas had wild mountain ancestors but now are used for their wool and to help people carry goods. Pumas are the top mountain **predator**.

CHAPTER 5
COUNTRIES AND CITIES

Brazil is the fifth-largest country in the world by size. It contains most of the Amazon River basin.

COUNTRIES

South America has 12 countries. The Falkland Islands, a **territory** of the United Kingdom, and French Guiana, an overseas region of France, are also part of South America.

Brazil has the most land of the South American countries. It covers nearly half of the continent. Brazil also has the most people. More than 200 million live there. Suriname is the smallest country. Fewer than 60,000 people live there. It also has the least amount of land of any South American country.

CITIES

More South Americans live in cities than in the countryside. For example, 95% of people in Uruguay make their homes in cities. Guyana is the only country where more people live in the countryside than in cities.

Montevideo is Uruguay's capital and also its largest city.

South America has five cities that have more than 10 million people. São Paulo, Brazil, is the largest. More than 20 million people live there. Life in a South American city is like any other big city. People live in apartments, go to work, and shop at supermarkets. But some people in cities are poor. They may have no power or running water.

CHAPTER 6
CULTURE AND PEOPLE

Indigenous peoples were the first to live in South American lands. Their civilizations date back thousands of years. Then explorers and settlers from Spain and Portugal came and took the Indigenous peoples' lands for their own. Today, the Indigenous peoples still fight for their rights.

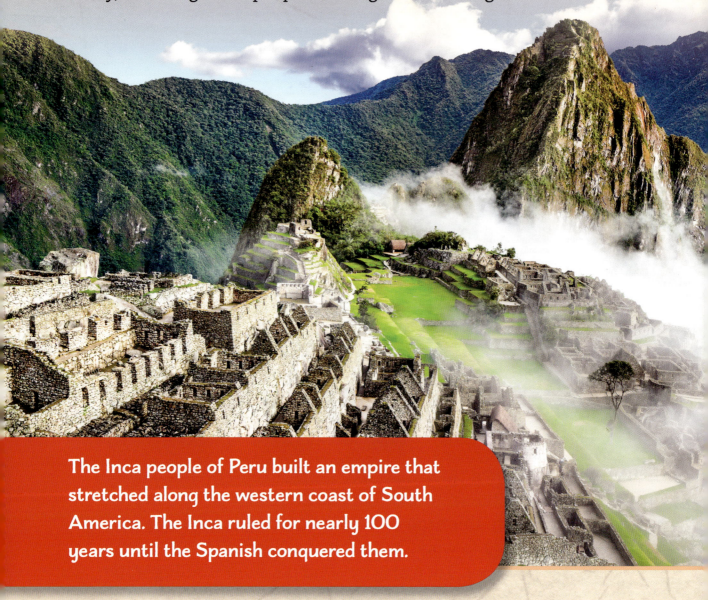

The Inca people of Peru built an empire that stretched along the western coast of South America. The Inca ruled for nearly 100 years until the Spanish conquered them.

Because Spain and Portugal settled much of South America, Spanish and Portuguese are the two most spoken languages. The settlers also brought their home cultures with them. But many Indigenous peoples kept their own traditions and languages. Millions speak Quechua, a language of the Andean region.

FOOD

Many South American countries have favorite foods. Argentinians enjoy hand-sized meat pies called empanadas. Ceviche, seafood prepared in fruit juice, is popular in Peru. Dulce de leche, a caramel spread, is loved all over the continent.

Empanadas are often filled with beef but can be made with many different fillings.

SPORTS

South Americans love sports. Argentinians enjoy watching polo, a sport played on horseback. Volleyball is popular in Brazil. But soccer is the most popular sport of all.

GLOSSARY

border (BOR-dr): The place where one area ends and another starts

carbon dioxide (KAR-bun dai-AHK-side): A gas made up of carbon and oxygen that people and animals breathe out of their lungs

climate (KLAI-muht): The usual weather conditions in a certain region or area.

equator (EE-kway-tr): An imaginary line around the middle of Earth that is the same distance from the North Pole to the South Pole

Indigenous (in-DIH-juh-nuhs): The first people who lived in any region and not later immigrants

plains (PLAYNZ): A large stretch of mostly flat land **predator** (PREH-duh-tr): An animal that lives by killing and eating other animals

species (SPEE-sheez or SPEE-sees): A group of animals or plants that are alike in certain ways

territory (TEH-ruh-tor-ee): Land controlled by or that belongs to a country

INDEX

Amazon rain forest 8, 12, 17-18

Andes 9, 11, 13, 14, 21

Brazil 11, 15, 17, 22, 23, 25, 29

Easter Island 7

Galápagos 7, 19

Indigenous 7, 26-27

jaguar 4, 18

Pampas 10, 15, 17, 20

toucan 4, 18

Uruguay 11, 24

COMPREHENSION QUESTIONS

1. How many people live in South America?
   a. More than 1 billion
   b. More than 400 million
   c. Fewer than 400,000

2. Which animal lives in the Amazon rain forest?
   a. Rhea
   b. Marine iguana
   c. Poison dart frog

3. What South American country has the most people?
   a. Brazil
   b. Venezuela
   c. Uruguay

4. True or False: All of South America lies below the equator.

5. True of False: The Amazon rain forest is the world's largest tropical rain forest.

Answers: 1. B, 2. C, 3. A, 4. False, 5. True

ABOUT THE AUTHOR

Tracy Vonder Brink loves true stories and facts. She has written more than 20 books for kids and is a contributing editor for three children's science magazines. Tracy lives in Cincinnati, Ohio, with her husband, two daughters, and two rescue dogs.

Written by: Tracy Vonder Brink
Cover design by: Kathy Walsh
Interior design by: Kathy Walsh
Series Development: James Earley
Proofreader: Crystal Sikkens
Educational Consultant: Marie Lemke M.Ed.
Print coordinator: Katherine Berti

Photographs: Shutterstock; Cover: ©Triff, ©Khurasan, ©nypl, @Dima_designer, ©Alberto Loyo; Title Pg: ©Triff, ©Dima_designer; Pg 3-31: ©Triff; Pg 4-31: ©RedKoala, © Sunny Whale; Pg 4: ©Delpixel; Pg 6: ©Anton_Ivanov; Pg 7: ©fl1photo; Pg 8: ©Anibal Trejo; Pg 9: ©kastianz; Pg 10: ©R.M. Nunes; Pg 11: ©worldclassphoto; Pg 12: ©Ondrej Prosicky; Pg 13: ©LAND; Pg 14: ©reisegraf.ch, ©vvoe; Pg 15: ©Alf Ribeiro; Pg 16: ©Dr Morley Read; Pg 17: ©Yatra; Pg 18: ©worldswildlifewonders, ©Roberts JS; Pg 19: ©FOTOGRIN, ©BlueOrange Studio; Pg 20: ©Uwe Bergwitz; Pg 21: ©Thorsten Spoerlein; Pg 22: ©dmitry_islentev; Pg 23: ©Danita Delimont; Pg 24: ©Globe Guide Media Inc; Pg 25: ©ESB Professional, Pg 26: ©cge2010; Pg 27: ©Yudina_Elena; Pg 28: ©Alexandr Vorobev; Pg 29: ©Debby Wong

Library and Archives Canada Cataloguing in Publication

Available at the Library and Archives Canada

Library of Congress Cataloging-in-Publication Data

Available at the Library of Congress

Crabtree Publishing Company
www.crabtreebooks.com   1-800-387-7650

Copyright © 2023 **CRABTREE PUBLISHING COMPANY**

All rights reserved. No part of this publication may be reproduced, stored in a retrieval system or be transmitted in any form or by any means, electronic, mechanical, photocopying, recording, or otherwise, without the prior written permission of Crabtree Publishing Company. In Canada: We acknowledge the financial support of the Government of Canada through the Canada Book Fund for our publishing activities.

Published in the United States
Crabtree Publishing
347 Fifth Avenue
Suite 1402-145
New York, NY, 10016

Published in Canada
Crabtree Publishing
616 Welland Ave.
St. Catharines, ON
L2M 5V6

Printed in the U.S.A./072022/CG20220201